THE FLOWER BOOK

Written by ANNE ORANGE
Illustrated by SHARON LERNER

LERNER PUBLICATIONS COMPANY
MINNEAPOLIS, MINNESOTA

CONTENTS

This year I planted a flower garden. First, I planted the seeds. Soon tiny plants poked their heads out of the ground. I watered them every day. I pulled out the weeds that grew around them.

The plants grew tall. Soon they had tiny buds. These buds became beautiful flowers. My flowers are so pretty. I want you to see them. Here are some of the flowers that grow in my garden.

DAISIES

My daisies have white petals. They have bright gold centers. Feel how soft the centers are.

Daisies close up their petals at night. They hide their gold centers. In the morning, the petals open up again to greet the sun.

Daisies are easy to grow. They are a nice garden flower. They grow wild in open fields, too. A green field full of bright daisies is so pretty in the spring!

TULIPS

The tulip flower looks like a little cup. It stands up straight and tall on its stem. Tulips come in many beautiful colors.

Tulips are grown from **bulbs**. A bulb looks like a small ball. Inside the bulb are tiny roots, stems, and leaves. I planted my tulip bulbs in the fall. All winter, the bulbs' roots grew. In early spring, the stems pushed out of the bulbs. They grew up through the ground and into the sunshine.

8

LILIES OF THE VALLEY

Many little white flowers grow on one stem. They look like tiny bells. Smell the flowers. How sweet they smell!

Lilies of the valley bloom only in April and May. But their leaves stay fresh and green all summer long.

Lilies of the valley are easy to grow. You can plant them in the sun or in the shade. Some people call these flowers May lilies.

ROSES

Roses are beautiful flowers. They grow best from small plants. I put some rose plants in my garden in the spring. I planted them in a sunny spot. I water them often. They need a lot of care.

Feel the stem of a rose. Watch out! Don't touch the sharp thorns! The thorns protect the rose from harm.

Mmmm—the roses smell so good. Perfume is often made from rose petals.

12

SUNFLOWERS

These are the biggest flowers growing in my garden. They have bright yellow petals and round brown centers.

Sunflowers grow very tall. They grow best in the hot sun. Watch a sunflower for a little while. You may see it move very slowly. It turns to follow the sun as the sun moves in the sky.

Sunflower seeds are not just for planting. They are good to eat, too!

GERANIUMS

My geraniums are red. Some geraniums are pink or white. Many little flowers grow on one geranium stem. All together, they make one geranium flower.

Geraniums grow best from **cuttings**. Cuttings are pieces of stem cut off a large plant. I put some geranium cuttings in water. I waited for them to grow roots. Then I planted the cuttings in the spring.

The geranium is one flower that is better to look at than to smell!

PANSIES

Touch a pansy's petals. They feel so soft. Pansies grow in many colors—purple, red, yellow, gold, light blue, and

18

brown. Look closely at a pansy. Do you see its little face? Spots of color give the face a smile.

DAFFODILS

My daffodils grew from bulbs, just like tulips. I planted daffodil bulbs in the fall, too. When spring came, they were the first flowers to bloom in my garden.

A daffodil has six bright yellow petals. Look at the part of the flower in the center of the petals. Does it stand taller than the petals? If it does, it is called a **trumpet**. It is called a **cup** if it is shorter than the petals.

SNAPDRAGONS

Many little snapdragon flowers grow on one stem. Bees like these flowers. They use the sweet nectar to make honey.

Snapdragon is a funny name for a flower. But look at one of the little flowers. It looks almost like a dragon's mouth. It has two lips. Press the sides of the snap-dragon together. The lips will open. Now let go. Snap! They come together again— just like the mouth of a tiny snapping dragon.

ZINNIAS

Many tiny petals make up one zinnia flower. Some zinnias are very small. Others are as big as grapefruit. Zinnias come in many beautiful colors.

I planted my zinnia seeds in the spring. They were not hard to grow. Zinnias will bloom in a sunny spot or in the shade. They will keep blooming all summer long.

You can pick as many zinnias as you want to. The more flowers you pick, the more will grow.

CHRYSANTHEMUMS

Chrysanthemums are beautiful flowers. Some people call these flowers "mums" for short. Most of them are bright yellow or gold.

You must plant chrysanthemum seeds in the spring. Then you will have to wait and wait. The flowers do not bloom until the end of summer. But you will be glad you waited when you see how pretty they are.

Pick some chrysanthemums. Put them in fresh water. They will look pretty for many, many days.

POPPIES

Feel the soft petals of a poppy. They are as thin as paper. My poppies are bright red. In their centers are small, round black seeds. These seeds taste good. Maybe you have eaten bread with poppy seeds on top.

Poppies grow best in sunny places. Many poppies grow wild. A field of red or gold poppies looks so pretty in the bright sunshine!

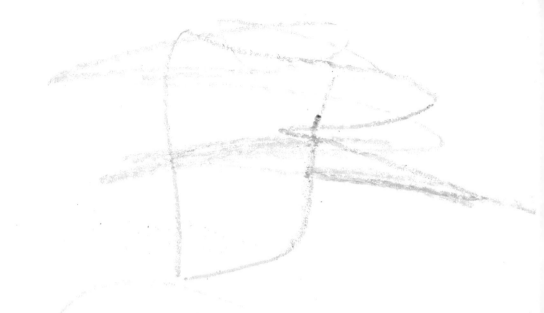

WHAT ARE YOUR FAVORITES?

So many beautiful flowers grow in my garden. Maybe you would like to plant some flowers yourself. You may have a special favorite.

Which flowers would you plant in your garden?

31

Children are curious. They enjoy learning about the familiar things around them—the fruits and vegetables they eat, the flowers they pick, or the trees that grow in their own neighborhoods. These books make such everyday things meaningful and interesting to children through the use of simple language and bright, bold illustrations. And each book may even inspire children to start collections, gardens, or art projects on their own.

THE FLOWER BOOK
THE VEGETABLE BOOK
THE LEAF BOOK
THE FRUIT BOOK

Young readers will also want to see these Art Concept books:

ORANGE IS A COLOR
SQUARE IS A SHAPE
STRAIGHT IS A LINE